3

FUN WITH
BARGELLO

FUN WITH BARGELLO

Mira Silverstein

CHARLES SCRIBNER'S SONS
New York

To Rose and Nathan Glassman

Acknowledgments:

I wish to thank Elinor Parker, my editor, for her help and encouragement and
for being one of the nicest people to work with.

Many thanks to Mr. Jacob Deschin, for technical advice and permission to use
his photographic equipment.

To my family, my deepest gratitude, for their understanding and cooperation
when I needed it most.

My thanks also to Selma Sundick, Rita Scheuer, Vivian Tanzer, Elise Silverstein, Shari Silverstein, Rona Amsterdam, Mildred Tobin, Audrey Karlan,
Harriette Gross, who worked the designs from my patterns.

All photographs by Salvator Lopes
Graph drawings by Elise Silverstein

Designs in Bargello by Mira Silverstein

I have prepared a small starter kit for beginners. It consists of small pieces of
mono canvas, assorted needles and a good selection of yarn, plus enough tape
for edging. For information write to: Needlecraft Boutique Ltd., 558 Middle
Neck Rd., Great Neck, L.I., N.Y. 11023.

Bargello embroidery is a type of needlework that has enjoyed renewed interest in recent years. Samples of this work have been found in the Bargello Museum in Florence, Italy. Therefore, Bargello embroidery is often referred to as Florentine needlework. Sometimes it is described as Flame stitch, or Hungarian point.

By any name, however, Bargello is one of the loveliest, most versatile of the needlepoint stitches, and by far the easiest to learn.

This book is prepared as a teaching guide for beginners, as well as an introduction to basic Bargello design.

Materials

Bargello can be worked on any open mesh, even-weave canvas or fabric with a variety of smooth even-textured yarns, such as tapestry wools, or cotton and silk embroidery threads. For the beginner, however, I suggest needlepoint single mesh (mono) canvas #12, #13 or #14, and a good quality tapestry or persian yarn. Do not use knitting worsted, since this is a softer yarn, and frays when worked through canvas. The finished work will tend to "pill" and will look shabby.

Use tapestry needles #17, #18, or #20 (the larger the number, the smaller the eye of the needle). Tapestry needles have a blunt point and a large, narrow eye for threading heavy yarns.

When purchasing materials, make certain that the yarn is of the proper weight in relation to the canvas you choose, and that the needle has an eye large enough to accommodate the yarn. Yet the eye must be slim enough to slide easily through the canvas holes. These materials and the proper assistance are easily obtained in any good needlecraft supply store, and will give most satisfactory results to anyone with little or no experience.

You will also need some masking tape to edge the rough edges of the canvas. This makes the canvas easier to handle and prevents it from ravelling. Do not use cellophane or surgical tape since the adhesive on these tapes gets a little messy when handled a lot and will make your needlework sticky. Machine stitching is another excellent way to edge canvas.

THE BEST WAY TO LEARN ANYTHING IS TO DO IT YOURSELF. So, why not begin right now? Get a small piece of canvas and a little yarn and a needle at the nearest needlecraft shop to prepare a small Bargello practice piece.

Edge the canvas. Thread the needle as follows: Fold yarn over needle and hold firmly between thumb and forefinger. Pull away needle without disturbing yarn. Keep pressing folded yarn between thumb and finger until yarn is very flat. Yarn should barely show. Rub the eye of the needle firmly over the fold. The needle is threaded in a wink.

Bargello embroidery is based on a simple upright stitch worked over a given number of canvas strands. Once the length of the stitch is established, the rest of the stitches should be of the same size. Start working from left to right (unless you are left-handed) and allow at least one inch margin on each side of the canvas.

Bring needle out in the left-hand corner, pull yarn out, count four STRANDS of canvas upward, and insert the needle directly opposite the point of exit. In the same continuous motion, return needle next to the original point of exit. You will find that you have completed a simple upright stitch. Repeat this several times, and work a number of stitches of equal size, side by side. For quick reference, we will refer to these as multiple stitches. Work a complete line of multiple stitches. Keep them even and smooth. Do not pull yarn too tight. Bargello needlework should look soft and fluffy. (See below)

Now try the next step: Begin a new line about an inch below the first one. This time work the stitch over four strands of canvas going up and two strands down (see page 10). Repeat this several times and you will notice that the effect is that of single steps going up from left to right. When the line is five steps high, reverse the procedure, counting four canvas strands down and two up. This time, you achieve a line of single steps going down from left to right. Repeat this exercise several times until the end of

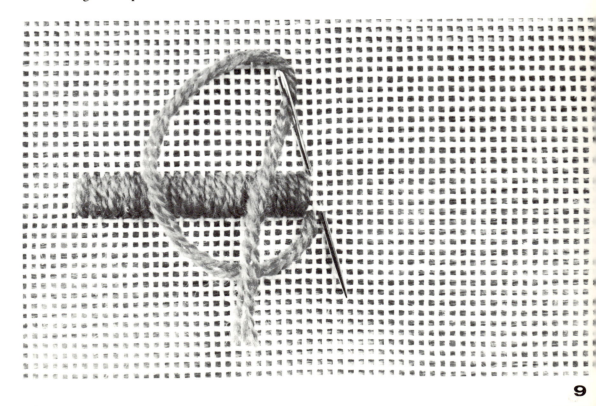

the line. This is the simplest Bargello "V" formation or "zigzag" design. For easier identification, we will call this stitch size a four and two. A longer stitch worked over six strands of canvas going up and three strands down, can be identified as six and three.

Practice some single lines. Study the samples on page 13 and copy them. Note that single step stitches in various combinations will give designs in V's and W's. By adding small groups of multiple stitches, you achieve round or oval effects. The larger the number of multiples

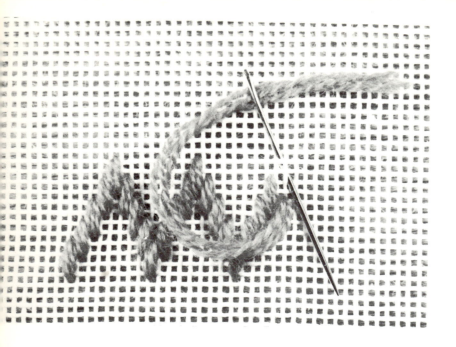

per line, the rounder your design will be. If you understand this, then you understand the principle of Bargello needlework.

Before we go any further, let me say a word about knotting. Don't. Learn from the very beginning to work without knots. When you start working on a new canvas, hold back about an inch of yarn on the wrong side. Hold it with your middle finger and work it under the first few stitches.

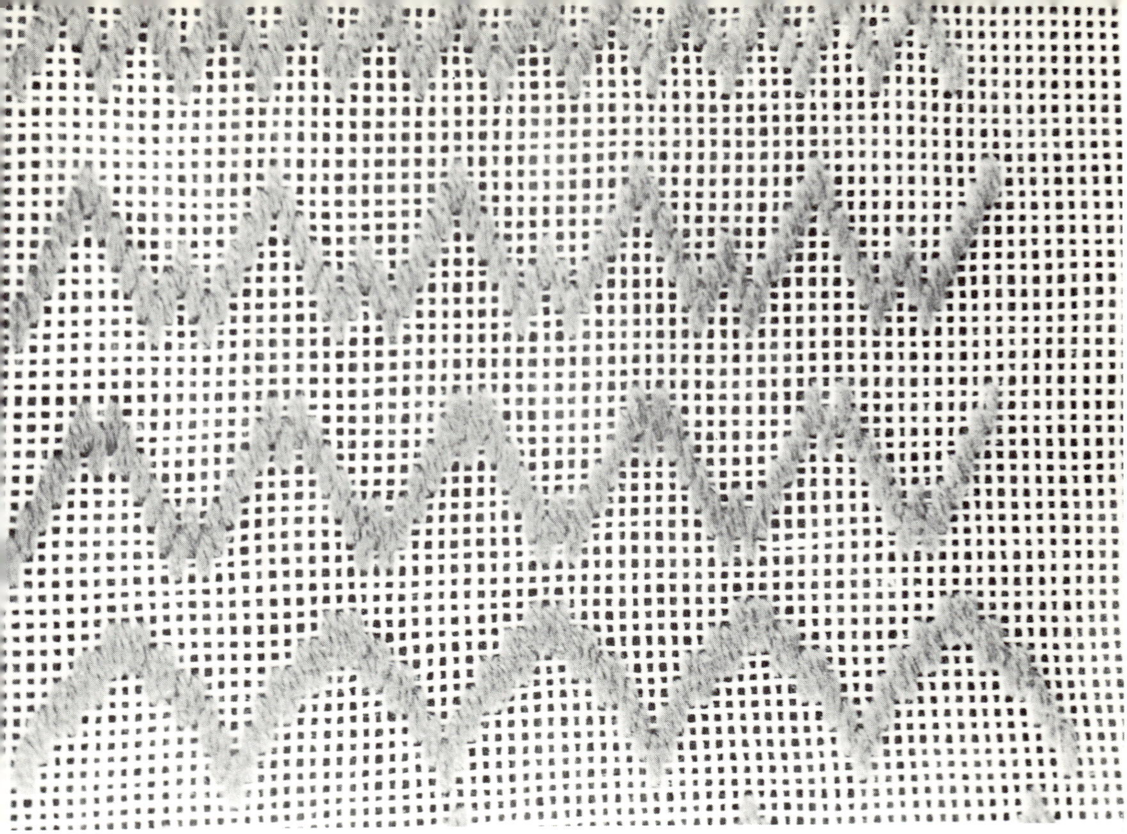

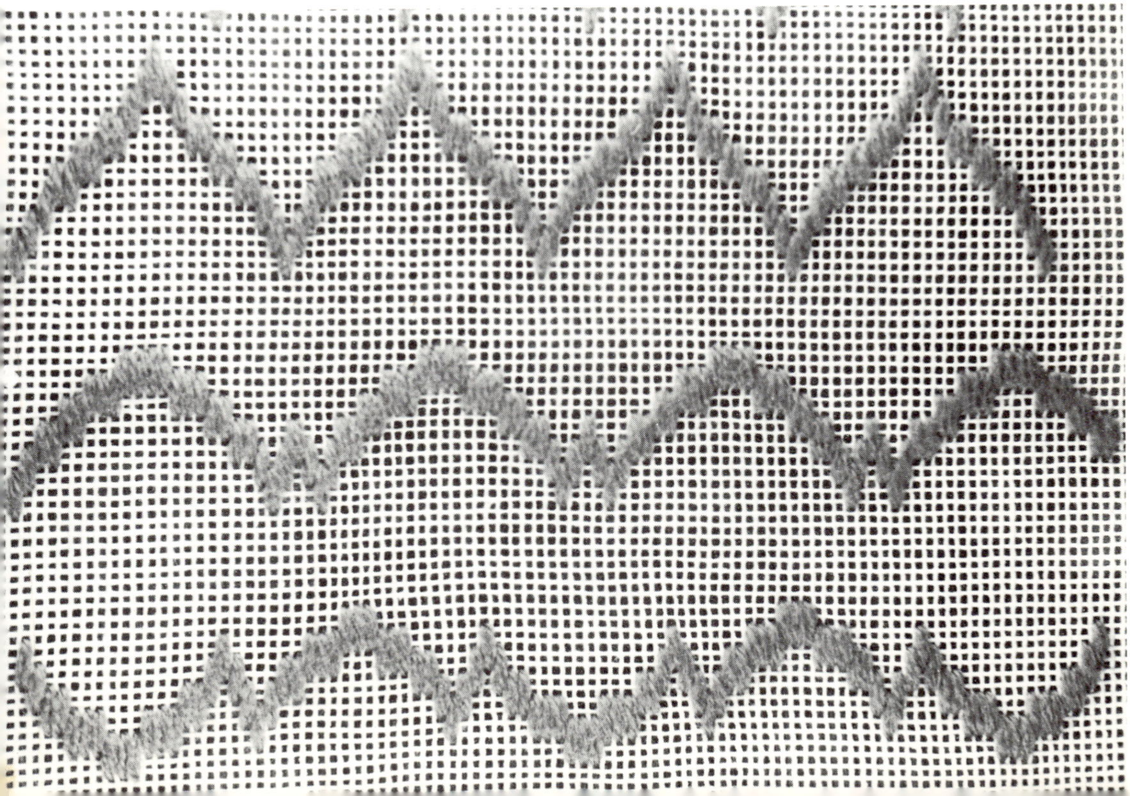

After the canvas is worked, it is a simple matter to start a new strand of yarn without knotting. Simply slip the threaded needle under several stitches on the wrong side of canvas. Do this at the nearest point of exit. Pull yarn through until the tail end is tucked under the back stitches, bring needle out on the right side of canvas and continue working. You finish off the yarn in the same manner, but in reverse. Keep all loose ends neatly trimmed on the back of the canvas to avoid tangled yarns.

To start a new line, begin directly below the first line (see ill.). If your stitch is over four strands of canvas, then count four strands below the FIRST STITCH. Bring threaded needle out and follow the lead line stitch by stitch. It is easier to use a different color for each new line until you gain more experience.

After each line is finished, and before you begin a new one, make sure that all points at top and bottom line up. Bargello is geometric in feeling and a mistake may throw the whole design out of line.

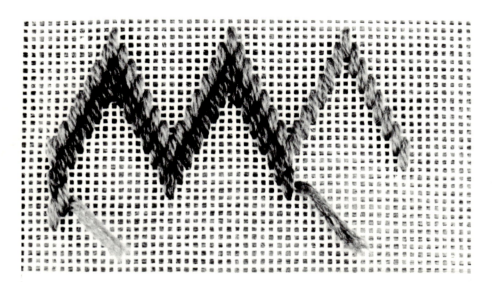

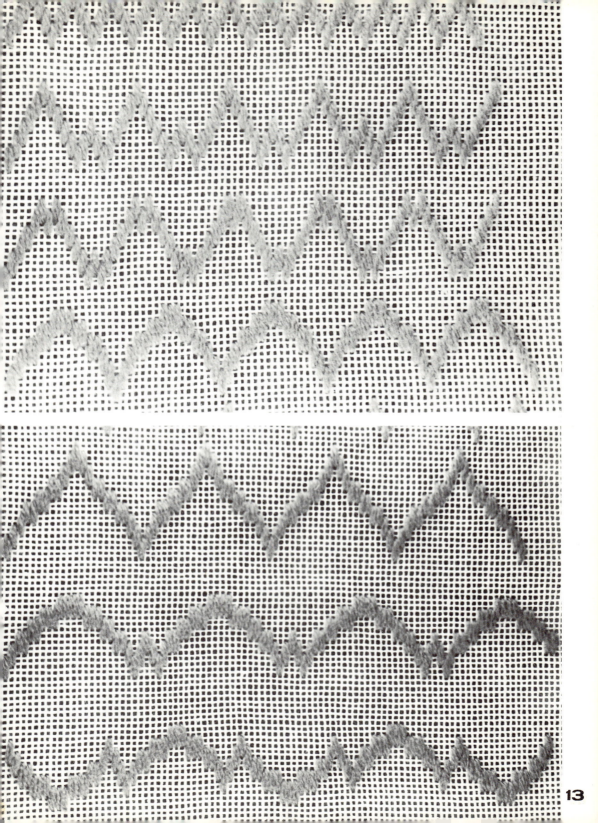

13

After the canvas is worked, it is a simple matter to start a new strand of yarn without knotting. Simply slip the threaded needle under several stitches on the wrong side of canvas. Do this at the nearest point of exit. Pull yarn through until the tail end is tucked under the back stitches, bring needle out on the right side of canvas and continue working. You finish off the yarn in the same manner, but in reverse. Keep all loose ends neatly trimmed on the back of the canvas to avoid tangled yarns.

To start a new line, begin directly below the first line (see ill.). If your stitch is over four strands of canvas, then count four strands below the FIRST STITCH. Bring threaded needle out and follow the lead line stitch by stitch. It is easier to use a different color for each new line until you gain more experience.

After each line is finished, and before you begin a new one, make sure that all points at top and bottom line up. Bargello is geometric in feeling and a mistake may throw the whole design out of line.

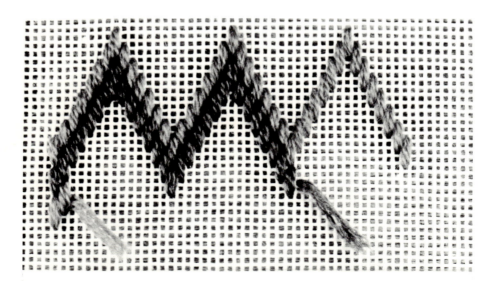

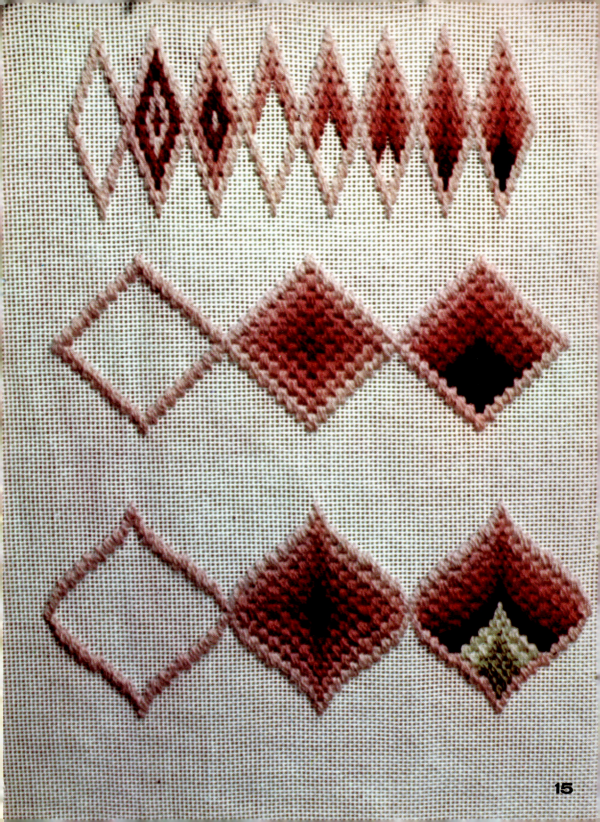

15

Establishing A Pattern

Select the size of canvas to be worked, and allow a margin of at least one inch on each side. Tape or machine stitch raw edges. Select your pattern and make sure you have enough yarn to finish the entire canvas. Not buying enough yarn is risky. Dye lots change continuously. Shops run out of supplies and colors may be discontinued without notice. So make sure you have enough yarn to finish with (read page 28 on estimating yarn).

Fold canvas in half and in half again. Press folds and open canvas. Pinpoint center where the folded lines cross, and begin there. Begin working with the *right half* of your pattern from the center point to the far right. End at margin. Return to center fold and finish the *left side* of

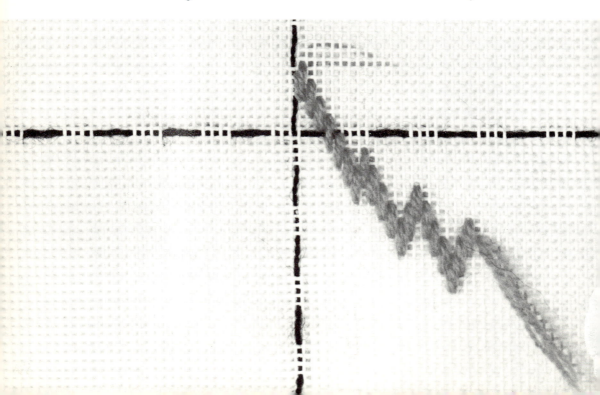

your pattern. Continue working to the left, and end at the margin. Turn canvas over so that you can work from left to right. Now that you have established your lead line, you work each line from left to right, straight across.

Make sure that your lead line is both accurate and well balanced. If your design is based on one lead line, establish your pattern on a given number of colors. You can use several shades in one family of colors, or you can use a seemingly wild combination of colors (see below). The fact that the pattern line repeats itself makes it pleasing to the eye. There is a certain uniformity in Bargello designs that makes them look right in a most modern setting, as well as in a traditional one.

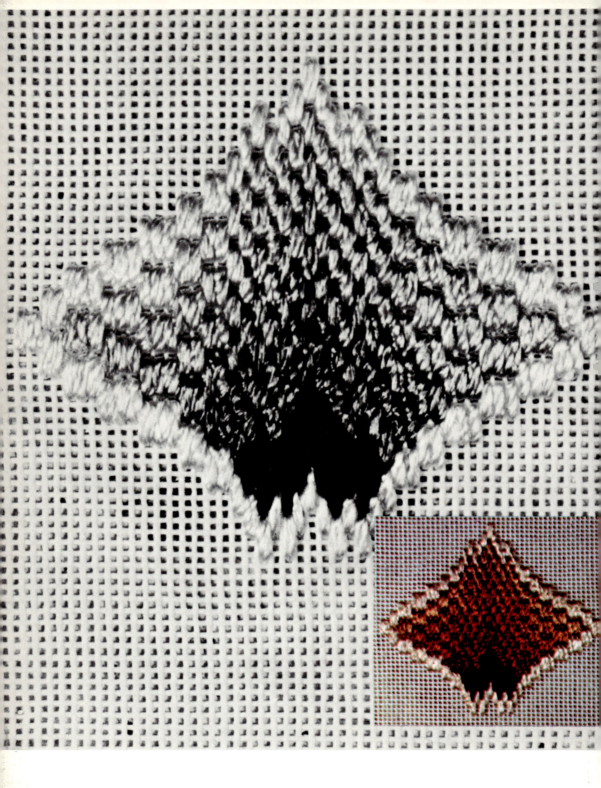

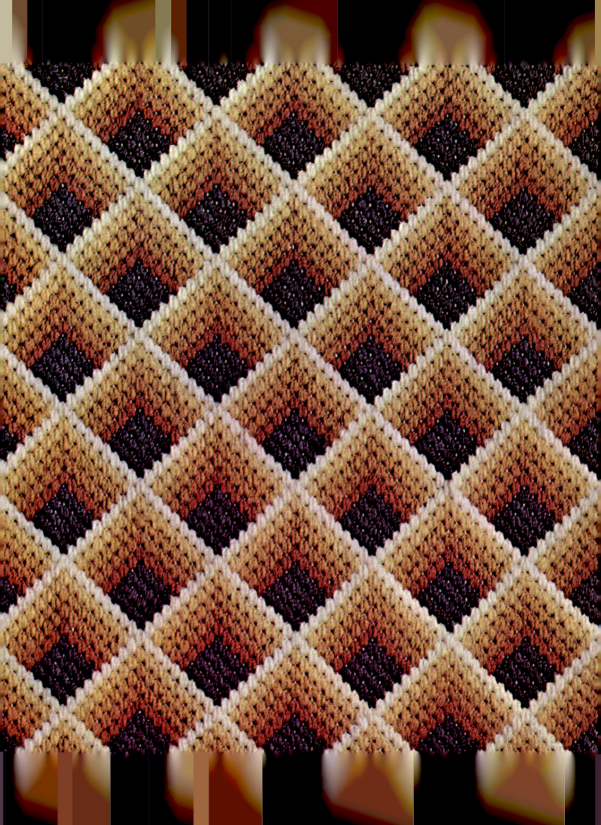

When the points of the Bargello design reach the margin line at the bottom, do not continue the design any further. Fill in areas between points with a series of diminishing inner lines until the pattern is squared off. Turn canvas around and finish the second half of the design.

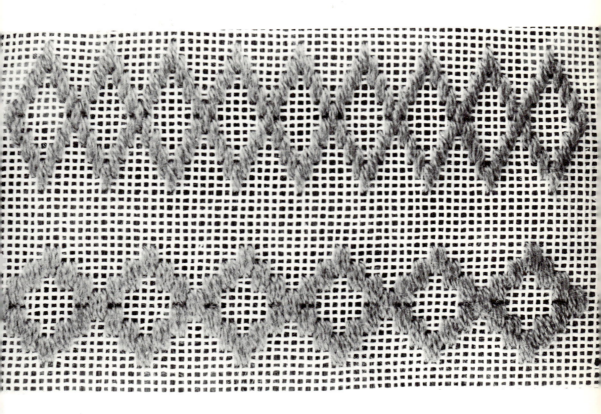

Patterned designs are easy to do if you follow a simple rule: do all the outline first. Once the outline is established, it is easy to balance the pattern and estimate your yarn. Also, there is a minimum amount of confusion since the most important counting is done, and all that is left is to fill in the patterns.

The patterns based on the diamond and persimmon designs (above and page 25) are the easiest and most versatile. Work up a lead line through the center of your

canvas as mentioned previously. Begin the second line
directly under the first one, but work it in reverse. Continue working one line at a time from left to right,
reversing every other one. When the entire canvas is
covered with the desired number of pattern outlines, fill in
one in the center with your choice of colors. This will
serve as a guide. Now, beginning at the top left-hand
corner, fill in all the patterns, using one color at a time.

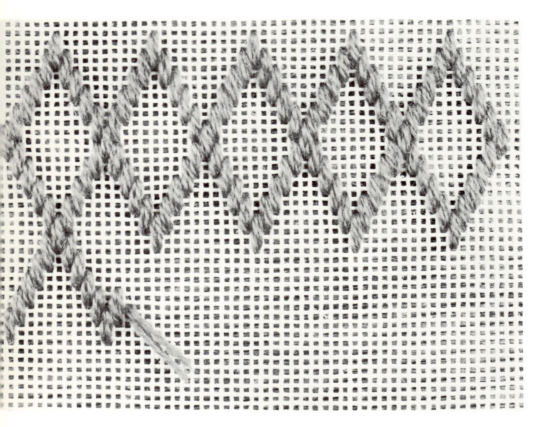

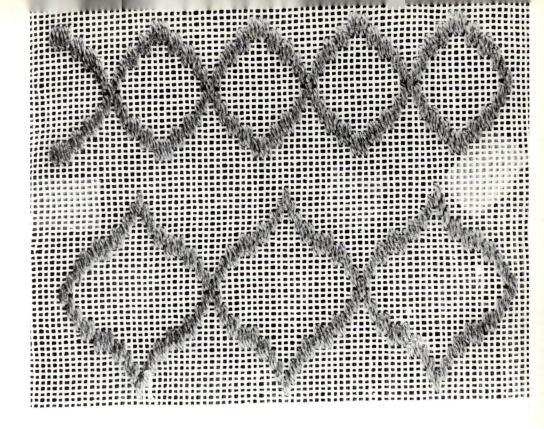

Three-dimensional designs

If you use the same method, you will find a three-dimensional design just as simple to do. The depth perception design in Bargello is an optical illusion. It is achieved by using several shades in close gradation in the same family of color. Page 15 illustrates precisely the depth perception look in Bargello. Choose any of the three patterns and work all the outlines in the lightest shade. Then, using a progressively darker shade, outline the inside UPPER HALF of the pattern one color at a time. Finish the lowest point in black or another contrasting color.

Practice all three samples on page 15. Enlarge or diminish patterns. Three-dimensional designs are excellent for floor pillows, foot stools, or small rugs worked with rug yarn on #3 canvas.

Estimating yarn is very important if you are going to do your own designs. Work up one line of Bargello in a given design. Count the number of strands it takes to do this. If you buy your yarn in skeins, cut them in equal strands of about 20 inches in length. If, for example, your stitch is 1/3 of an inch long, you will get three lines of Bargello to one inch of canvas or 45 lines to 15 inches of canvas. Assuming your line is 15 inches across, and you used 4 strands of yarn to finish it, then: 4 x 45 = 180. If you use 6 different shades in equal amounts then: 180 ÷ 6 = 30 you will need thirty strands in each color. Add 10% extra to allow for errors.

To estimate yarn for patterns, work up several complete patterns using up at least one ten strand skein of yarn in each color. Measure one completed pattern in width and in length, and figure out how many of them will fit into your canvas. If, for example, you were able to finish two complete patterns using one skein of yarn in each color, and you have 30 patterns to finish, then you will need 15 skeins in each color. Add 10% for good measure. Left-over yarn never goes to waste. Keep each color separate in a box or basket rather than a bag. Use it whenever you are in the mood to try out new design ideas.

Brick stitch is a simple Bargello design that lends itself to many lovely effects. It is worked from left to right, as well as right to left. The reverse side of the brick

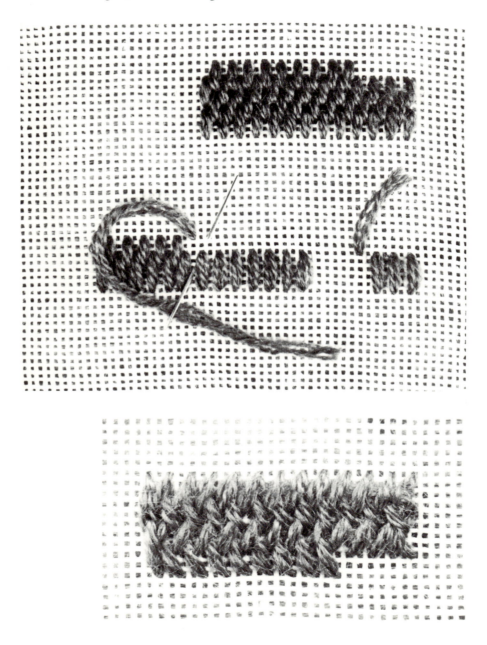

A sample showing double brick stitch.

stitch presents a close weave (page 32, bottom) which makes it most suitable for chair seat covers, or small rugs (see page 26, bottom).

Two variations on Bargello needlework: below, stitch is worked over six strands of canvas going up and five strands down, the steps raised and lowered one strand

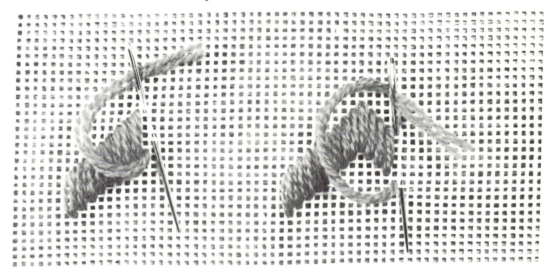

Lines of the same depth worked over 6 threads. Bottom photo on page 35 shows the same design worked over 7, 3 and 2 threads. (See Fig. 4)

of canvas at a time instead of two. This design can be worked over any number of strands in rows of different widths (page 35, A). Several design ideas appear on the following pages. B is worked as follows: the first stitch over four strands up—down one—up two—down one—up four. Repeat ending with a four strand stitch. This gives you a line of long and short stitches. On the second line begin

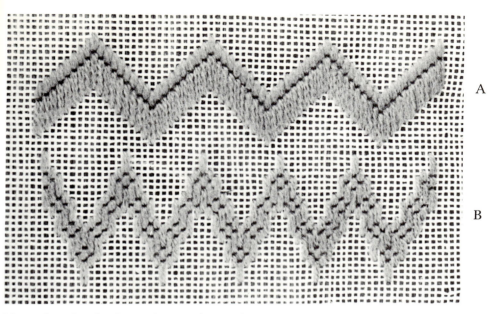

A

B

Lines of varying depths can be more interesting.

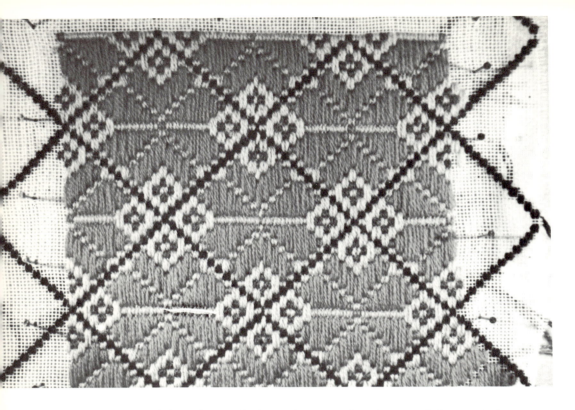

with a short stitch. Make sure that long and short stitches alternate. Try a small sample and work up several lines. Make sure you master it before you attempt anything more elaborate. This design, incidentally, is marvellous when used as background, especially when you have to cover a large blank area.

The design above in red, green and black is very striking. Colors can be changed for a softer look. Designs on page 27 and 31 are suggested for samplers. These are more interesting than the customary checkerboard pattern often used. Patterns can be interchanged or you can make your own.

Throughout the book are a number of Bargello designs in color. These are only a small sampling of the unlimited possibilities in store for you. The outline graphs start on page 39 and you can follow them easily. However, you will have more fun changing colors and experimenting with your own design ideas.

A few final words on Bargello embroidery. Use only the finest materials. The difference in cost is negligible, and a good quality canvas will hold up better. Fine yarns are color-fast, moth-proof, and come in a large range of exciting colors that stay bright and fresh for years.

Do not use markers of any kind on Bargello canvas. Counting strands is more accurate and most marking pens will run into the wool when wet. If you must indicate a margin, use a running stitch in left-over yarn.

Bargello does not need blocking, but it should be fluffed and squared after it is finished. Wet finished piece in cold water (assuming you used color-fast yarns). Place Bargello right-side-up on a flat board over a towel. Pull sides gently to square. The wool will fluff out. Use push-pins or small nails to hold the canvas flat. Do not press. Let it dry away from artificial heat. When the Bargello is completely dry, remove it from the board and finish it into something pretty, such as a handbag, a pillow, chair seat cover, or frame it.

Have fun with Bargello.

A belt in three colors, worked longitudinally. (See Fig. 9)

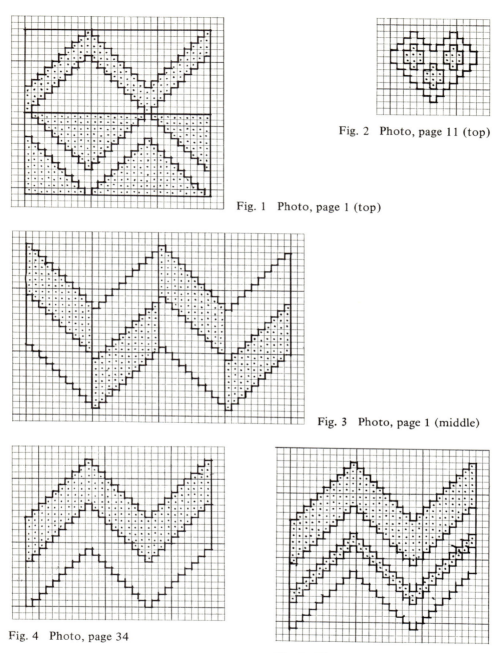

Fig. 1   Photo, page 1 (top)

Fig. 2   Photo, page 11 (top)

Fig. 3   Photo, page 1 (middle)

Fig. 4   Photo, page 34

Fig. 5   Photo, page 35 (bottom)

On the graphs, the number of boxes between the lines is the number of threads you count on the canvas.

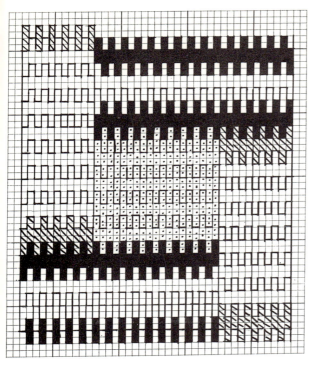

Fig. 6 Photo, page 26 (bottom)

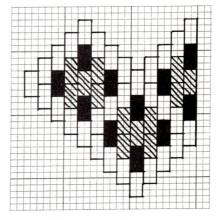

Fig. 7 Photo, page 12

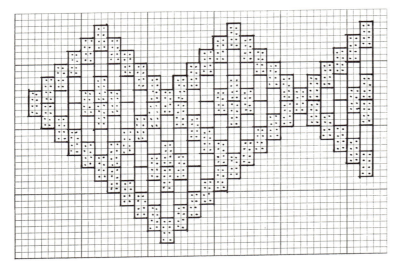

Fig. 8 Photo, page 33

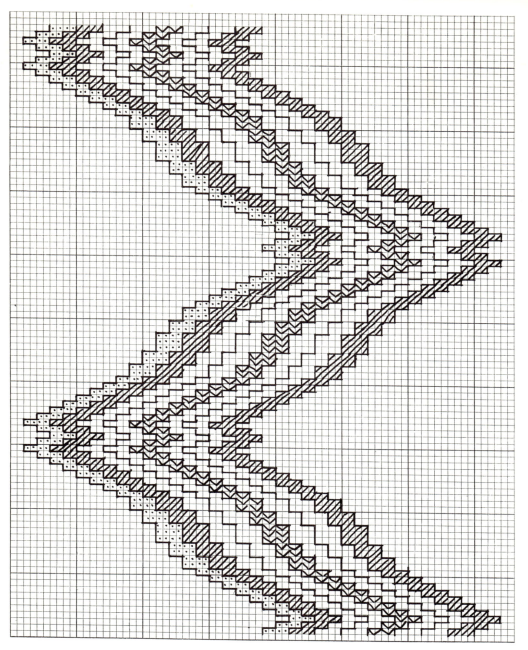

Fig. 9   Photo, page 26 (top)

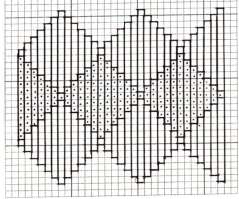

Fig. 10   Photo, above

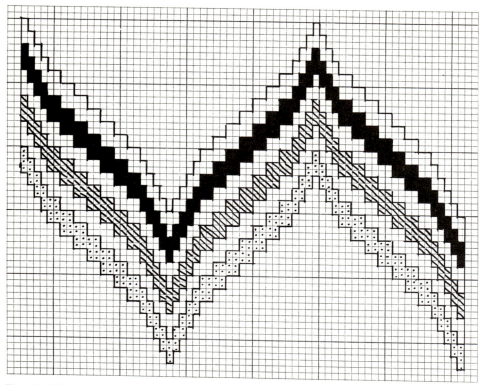

Fig. 11   Photos, pages 17 and 20

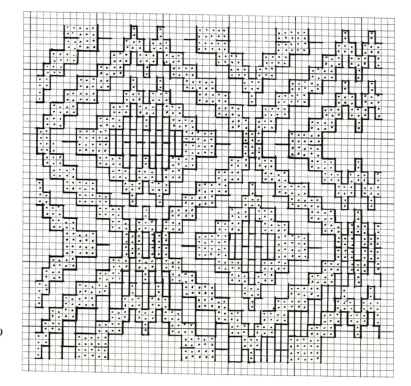

Fig. 12
Photo, page 29

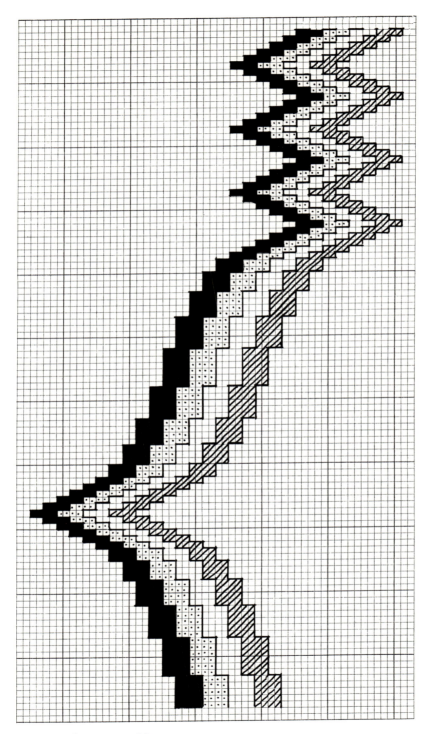

Fig. 13   Photo, page 22

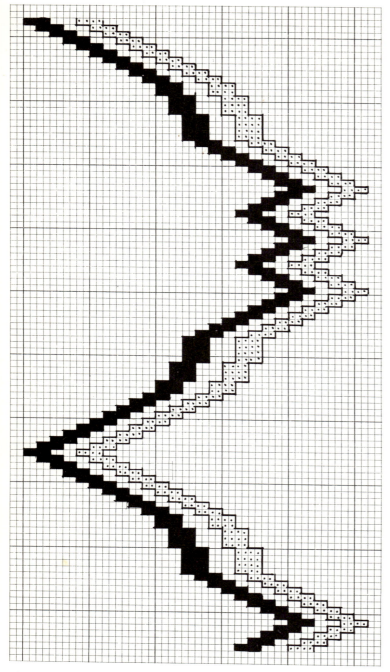

Fig. 14   Photo, page 23

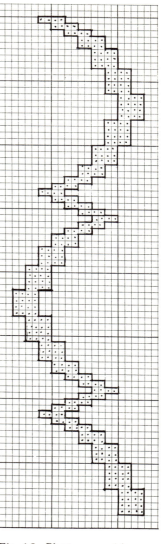

Fig. 15   Photo, page 11

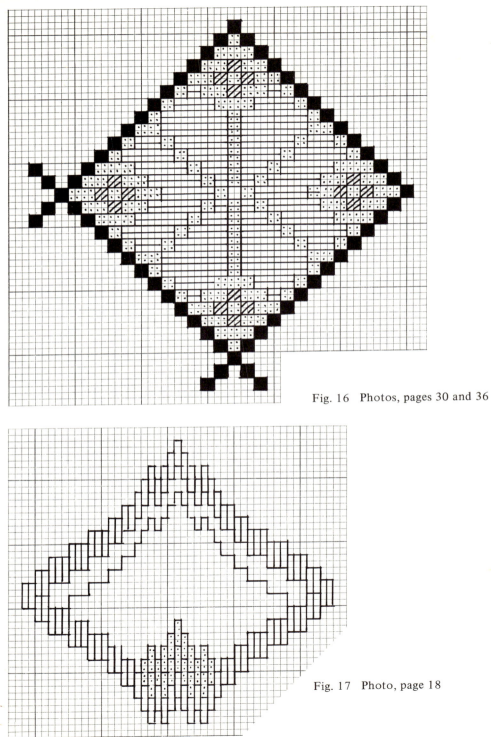

Fig. 16   Photos, pages 30 and 36

Fig. 17   Photo, page 18

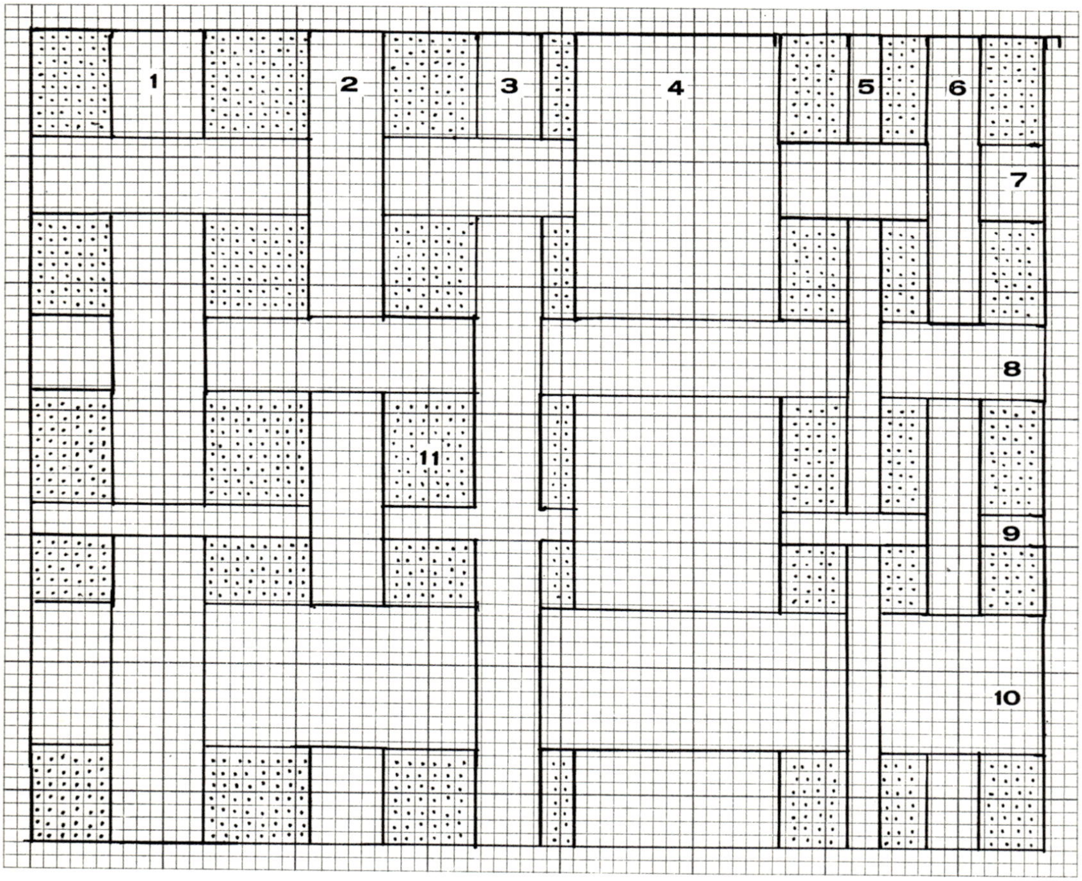

Fig. 18 Photo, page 31
(On this graph 1 square = 2 stitches)

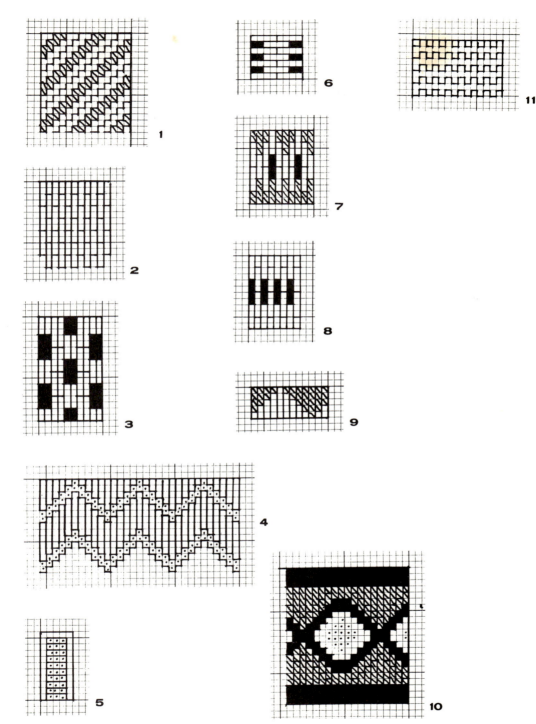

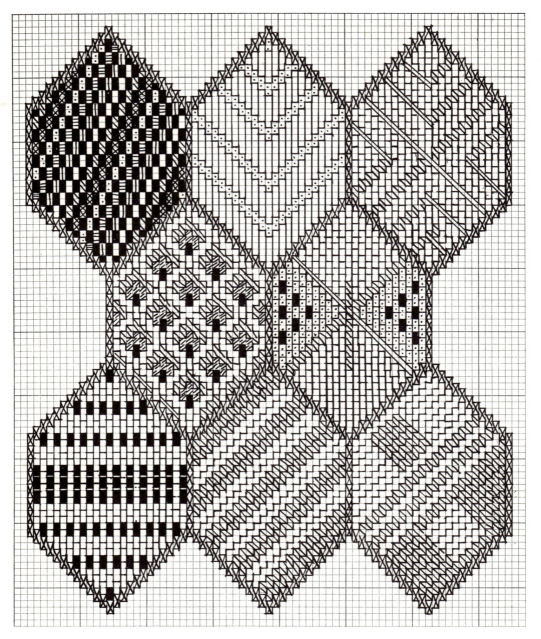

Fig. 19 Photo, page 27